Silent Sound

By the Same Author

COLONIES IN ORBIT
The Coming Age of Human Settlements in Space

EAVESDROPPING ON SPACE
The Quest of Radio Astronomy

GALAXIES, ISLANDS IN SPACE

HARNESSING THE SUN
The Story of Solar Energy

THE MOONS OF OUR SOLAR SYSTEM
Newly Revised Edition

THE TINY PLANETS
Asteroids of Our Solar System

A Navy frogman tests new ultrasonic sonar equipment designed to locate objects underwater. Earphones provide the diver with audio information about objects detected by the searching sonar beam.

SILENT SOUND

The World of Ultrasonics

by David C. Knight

ILLUSTRATED WITH PHOTOGRAPHS AND DIAGRAMS

William Morrow and Company
New York   1980

Printed in the United States of America.
1   2   3   4   5   6   7   8   9   10

Library of Congress Cataloging in Publication Data

Knight, David C
   Silent sound.
   Includes index.
   Summary: Examines extremely high frequency sound known as
ultrasound and discusses its use in navigation, industry, and medicine.
   1. Ultrasonics—Juvenile literature. [1. Ultrasonics. 2. Sound] I.
Title.
QC244.K53   534.5′5   80-19118
ISBN 0-688-22244-7
ISBN 0-688-32244-1 (lib. bdg.)

Permission for use of photographs gratefully acknowledged: Automa-
tion Industries/Sperry Division, page 41 top; Branson/a SmithKline
Company, pages 47, 50, 52; Dentsply International, page 83; Metzler
Ultrasonics, page 78; Panametrics, Incorporated, pages 24, 41 bottom,
44, 45; Raytheon Company, page 36; RCA, page 34; Searle Ultrasound, pages 24, 71, 72; United States Navy, page 32; Wave Energy
Systems, Incorporated, pages 49, 88; Westinghouse Corporation,
pages 48, 53.

Contents

Silent Sound

1
What Is Ultrasonics?

The next time you walk down a country road in the summertime or sit in someone's backyard, stop whatever you are doing and listen. If there are no man-made noises to drown it out, you will hear the constant, drowsy murmur of chirping crickets, droning flies, singing grasshoppers, and humming bees.

Even as you listen to these thin, faint noises, some of these insects are making a great many *other* sounds that no human ear can detect. It is thought that many kinds of insects communicate with each other by means of silent sound—silent, that is, to us. In recent years scientists have succeeded in inventing ingenious instruments for picking up these sounds and for using them as a powerful tool.

The study of such sounds is called "ultrasonics" (*ultra* meaning "beyond," and *sonics* meaning "sound"). The term *supersonics* was formerly applied to this field, but that word is now used to describe speeds exceeding that of sound through the air—about one mile every five seconds. For example, people refer to the Concorde as a supersonic plane, meaning it can fly faster than sound can travel through the air.

The difference between ultrasonic waves—or *ultrasound*—and ordinary sound waves is a matter of frequency. What exactly *is* frequency? Imagine a vibrating object, say a tuning fork, sending out sound waves in all directions. The waves travel outward in ever-widening "shells," one inside the other. If you could see the sound waves made by the tuning fork, they would look something like round balloons of different sizes, one inside the other. The balloons represent the compressions, and the spaces between them represent the expansions, of the air molecules through which the sound waves travel.

When the molecules are pushed together by the for-

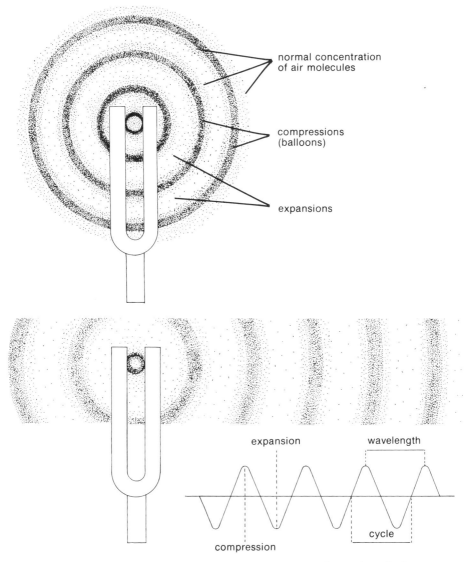

normal concentration
of air molecules

compressions
(balloons)

expansions

expansion

wavelength

compression

cycle

Sound waves being created in air by a struck tuning fork.
Waves travel as a series of compressions and expansions. A
cycle is one compression and one expansion. Wavelength is
the distance from one compression to the next.

13

ward vibrating action of the tuning fork, they are compressed; when they are pulled away by the backward action of the fork, they are spread apart, or expanded. Think of the tuning fork—the source of the sound—as in the center of all the balloons.

Sound travels because this double motion affects the molecules making up air ever farther and farther away from the source of the sound. Thus, sound waves are a series of compressions and expansions in whatever medium—usually air—that surrounds them and through which they travel. The word *cycle* is used to mean one compression and one expansion. Sound waves are made up of such cycles, or times. An object that vibrates 500 times each second causes 500 compressions and 500 expansions each second. In other words, it vibrates at the rate of 500 cycles a second. The number of cycles per second is called the "frequency" of the sound waves.

A sound wave in which the molecules of the medium vibrate comparatively slowly has a low frequency. A wave of 200 cycles per second, for instance, is considered a low-frequency wave. A wave in which the molecules vibrate very fast, say, 10,000 cycles per second, has a high frequency.

Why does frequency differentiate ultrasonic from ordinary sound waves? Because the human ear is so constructed that even at its keenest threshold of hearing it can register as sound only frequencies that lie between 16 and 16,000 times, or cycles, per second. Ultrasonics, or ultrasound, is chiefly concerned with the frequencies above 16,000. Scientists have made studies of the lower range, which is called "infrasound," but ultrasound is by far the more interesting and important to them.

It is known that certain kinds of grasshoppers can produce ultrasound with a frequency of 40,000 cycles. Small animals such as rats, guinea pigs, and cats register frequencies up to 30,000 and perhaps even higher. Some people call their dogs with a special "silent" whistle. It is so high that human beings cannot hear it, but the dogs, whose threshold of hearing is higher than that of people, can hear the whistle and respond to it.

Few members of the animal kingdom are as dependent on ultrasound as bats. Experiments with these creatures have proved that their inner ears are so delicately constructed that they can hear frequencies as high as 100,000 cycles per second. This ability was discovered when zoologists—scientists who study animals—solved a question that had long baffled them: What enables bats, which fly about in the dark hours of the night, to avoid bumping into obstacles such as cave walls and tree branches?

First the scientists developed a device by which any high-frequency sounds produced by the bats could be picked up. Then a number of bats were masked and made

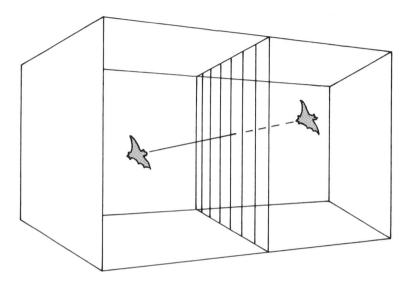

Scientists tested bat sonar in a room strung with wires.

to fly through a room in which wires were hung from the ceiling only a foot apart. As long as the wires used were not extremely thin, the masked bats avoided them easily. The device revealed that a bat in flight produces ultrasound squeaks or cries, which are echoed from any object in the bat's path and picked up by its ears. Thus, the bat is warned ahead of time of possible collisions and can quickly change its direction of flight.

As a bat nears some obstacle, it may give as many as

thirty to fifty of these cries per second. To prove that these echoes guide the bats, the scientists gagged their mouths and stopped their ears in addition to masking their eyes. Under these new conditions, the bats blundered helplessly into the wires and even crashed into the walls of the room.

Follow-up experiments showed that each bat cry consists of about 100 individual sound waves. These waves crowd together as each cry begins and then spread farther apart toward the end of the cry. The frequency of the waves ranges from 100,000 or higher at the beginning of the cry to about 40,000 or slightly lower at the end. Experts think that the longer interval between vibrations at the end of the cry enable the bat to hear the echoes from the first part of the cry. Incidentally, like bats in flight, dolphins and white whales also have a built-in echo-return system, which they use to locate fish and obstacles in the water.

At this point, one might well ask why the bats' cries need to be of such high frequency. The answer, which helps explain one of the uses of ultrasonics to human beings, concerns the wavelengths of sounds.

Remember that a sound wave traveling through a medium such as air or water is a series of compressions and expansions. These waves are also known as longitudinal waves, because they are propagated, or transmitted, by compression and tension of particles (the molecules in air) moving parallel to the direction of the wave impulse. The wave*length* of a sound is the distance from one compression to the next (see diagram on page 13). When the wavelength is relatively long, the sound flows around small obstacles, much as a large ocean wave flows around a buoy, with scarcely any disturbance of the water in which it is anchored. (This ability of any sort of long wave—whether it be sound or light or radio —to spread around an object is called "diffraction.")

In the case of short wavelengths, however, the sound is bounced back, or echoed, from small objects, just as tiny wavelets in calmer ocean water bounce or splash back from the buoy. In other words, short wavelengths are diffracted less—if at all—than long wavelengths. For this reason, the high-frequency cries of bats, which have very short wavelengths, echo back from objects such as slender wires—provided they aren't hair thin—and the bats are safely guided around unseen obstacles.

Because ultrasonic waves have a very short wavelength, many of them—and their energy—are packed into a small space. Ordinary sound waves move outward in all directions; while they have energy, it is usually rather weak. It has been estimated that a million persons talking steadily for an hour and a half in a huge hall would produce only enough sound energy, converted to heat, to heat a single cup of tea. But the shortness of ultrasonic wavelengths means they can be focused in a narrow, straight, beam. When they are, concentrated energy of tremendous power is created.

This power of ultrasound has been demonstrated in research laboratories time and again. In one experiment, ultrasonic waves from a whistle are focused to a point of high intensity by means of a concave reflector upon some cotton, as in the accompanying picture. The concentrated waves cause the cotton fibers to vibrate so rapidly that a fire is started from friction. In another test,

Ultrasonic waves are focused upon some cotton; the waves agitate the cotton fibers so rapidly that a fire starts by friction.

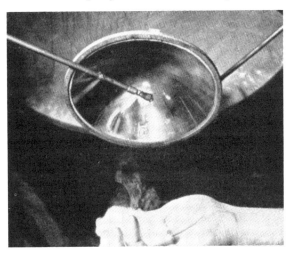

ultrasonic waves with a frequency of one million cycles pass through water in which an egg has been placed. The energy of the waves breaks down the contents of the egg and cooks it—without breaking the shell. In still another test, ultrasonic waves with a frequency of almost three million cycles are sent through a tank of water. Slowly a mound forms on the surface. So violent is the force that the water froths like boiling lava in an active volcano. At length, droplets of water fly up from the mound and produce a fountain several inches high.

This great power of ultrasound has been known for

Ultrasonic waves with a frequency of three million cycles producing a fountain effect in a tank of water

many years, but practical applications of it are only of recent date. Today scientists are increasingly finding ways of putting this concentrated energy to use in scientific research, military equipment, industry, and in biology and medicine.

Various ways of producing ultrasonic waves have been discovered so that they can be put to effective use. The one most used for sending ultrasound through solids or liquids depends on a peculiar property of certain crystals such as quartz. This property, first discovered and studied by Pierre Curie in 1880, is called the "piezoelectric effect." The term comes from the Greek word *piezein,* meaning "to press," and *electric*; it is also known as the pressure-electric phenomenon.

Here is how the effect works: When pressure applied by weights is brought to bear on a quartz-crystal plate cut in a certain way, the crystal becomes electrically charged. The more pressure, or mechanical stress, that is applied, the greater the current that is generated. Now if the crystal is suddenly stretched instead of being pressed, the charge will reverse itself. By alternately stretching and compressing the crystal, an alternating current is set up. If an alternating current of the same frequency as the crystal's natural one is applied to the crystal, it will expand and contract in rhythm with the changes in the direction of the current.

21

Thus, by applying electricity to a crystal, ultrasonic waves are created. In many cases, small metal plates are attached to the crystal in an ultrasonic device, and these plates move up and down in the same rhythm. This motion, in turn, sets up similar vibrations (the ultrasonic waves) in the medium—often light oil—in which the device is immersed. By cutting the crystal to a certain length and thickness, the ultrasonic waves are made to travel in a longitudinal direction, that is, along the direction of the beam of sound. However, there are other crystal cuts in which the waves can be made to travel at right angles to the direction of the beam.

Another method of producing ultrasonic waves is by magnetostriction, a term coming from the word *magneto* or *magnetic* plus the Latin word *strictio*, meaning "a drawing together." Magnetostriction simply means a change in the dimensions of a body when it is magnetized.

Magnetostriction for the creation of ultrasound involves the use of an iron or nickel rod. Around the rod is placed a solenoid, a tubular coil for the production of a magnetic field. When a high-frequency alternating current is sent through the solenoid, the rod is magnetized in such a way that its atoms are distorted and, therefore, its dimensions changed. These tiny expansions and contractions then set up ultrasonic vibrations that are communicated to whatever medium surrounds the rod.

A third method of creating ultrasound is by whistle or siren-type generators. These devices utilize streams of gas or liquids at high velocities in connection with resonant cavities or reflectors. The frequency of the vibrations produced is determined by the natural sound velocity in the particular liquid gas that is used.

Here it should be pointed out that the field of ultrasonics is concerned not with one type of high-frequency sound wave but with three. At present, the longitudinal wave, which can be focused into a powerful beam, is the most important one commercially. A second type is the transverse wave, whose molecules move up and down at right angles to the wave direction, setting up shear stresses between them. Certain crystal cuts will produce such waves, and they can be focused, but not with the efficiency of longtitudinal waves. A third type is the surface wave which is somewhat like a water wave. These waves are propagated by an up-and-down motion as well as by an expansive molecular motion on the surface of the carrying medium. Thus, engineers and scientists have a choice of sound waves, each of which can be used to perform various tasks ultrasonically.

Whatever method is used to produce ultrasound—and whichever type of wave is selected to do a particular job —the assembly or device that creates the high-frequency waves is called an "ultrasonic transducer." A transducer

is any instrument that transforms one kind of energy into another. In the case of magnetostrictive and piezoelectric transducers, electrical energy is transformed into sound, or mechanical, energy. Transducers are also known as sound heads.

In general, the magnetostrictive transducer made entirely of metal is the most rugged and trouble-proof. However, it is the least efficient as it requires much higher electrical power to deliver the same amount of energy as a ceramic piezoelectric transducer. While the piezoelectric transducer is the most efficient, it is the least rugged and deteriorates quickly in high heat.

Although many applications of ultrasonic vibrations have been devised, the use of ultrasound is a relatively new science. Each year new ways to harness this power are being discovered, and they hold much promise for the future.

Modern ultrasonic transducers come in many shapes and sizes. At left, are standard contact transducers. At right, disassembled and assembled, a transducer used in a diagnostic ultrasound unit.

2

In the Sea

As early as World War I, a French scientist named Dr. Paul Langevin found a way to make use of the echoing property of ultrasonic waves. At France's major naval base at Toulon on the Mediterranean Sea, he and his assistants constructed an apparatus that could send strong bursts of high-frequency sound waves through the water. Adapting the piezoelectric technique of Pierre Curie, he sandwiched slabs of quartz between steel plates and sent

26

alternating current through the quartz. The current forced the quartz to vibrate, inducing sound waves of the same frequency in the water.

The ultrasonic waves produced by Dr. Langevin traveled in straight paths without being diffracted and so returned to their origin. Langevin's work came too late in the war to be of much use militarily, but it pointed the way toward the development of sonar in World War II.

Langevin also experimented with the effect of ultrasonic waves on marine life. He discovered that small fish swimming through his ultrasonic beams were killed instantly. When one of his assistants held his hand in the path of the waves for a brief instant, he felt an agonizing pain, as if his very bones were being heated. These experiments forcefully brought home to Langevin the potentially powerful energy with which he was dealing. However, it remained for others to develop it more fully.

After World War I, some Canadian scientists applied Dr. Langevin's discoveries to their own work. In time, they developed a device for locating treacherous icebergs and hidden reefs. It was another precursor of sonar.

Sonar, developed during World War II, was a much greater refinement of the earlier ultrasonic underwater devices. Indeed, it had a great deal to do with the conquest of the dreaded wolf packs of German submarines that roamed the Atlantic Ocean early in the war. The word *sonar* is an American acronym for *so*und *n*avigation *a*nd *r*anging. The British equivalent is *asdic*, for *A*nti-*S*ubmarine *D*etection *C*ommittee. Primarily a military device, sonar is used for underwater observation, communication, and detection. Sonars are an essential part of present-day naval equipment to detect and identify enemy vessels preparatory to an attack.

Sonar works in this way. When a pulse of ultrasonic waves is beamed through the water from a ship equipped with sonar, an echo of the same frequency is reflected back to the sonar apparatus from any solid object in the path of the waves. Since the waves are not diffracted, the direction from which the echo returns reveals the position of the object. The distance, for example, of a submarine from the sonar-equipped ship can be calculated from the length of time that elapsed between the sending of the original pulse and the return of the echo. Actually, such calculations are done electronically by the apparatus, and it is able to repeat the transmitting and receiving operations many times per second so that extremely brief periods of time may be measured. The sonar receiver converts the reflected signal into either an audible *pinging* sound, an image on an oscilloscope screen, or a marking on a roll of chart paper for the sonar operator's convenience.

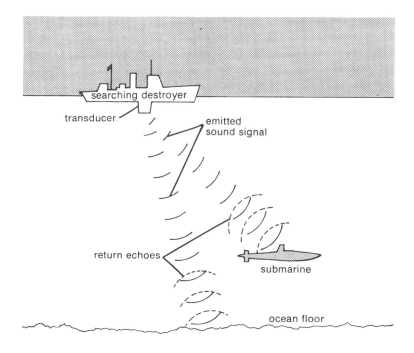

transducer

searching destroyer

emitted
sound signal

return echoes

submarine

ocean floor

Sonar locates underwater objects by means of reflected sound waves. The transducer converts electrical impulses into sound pulses for transmission through the water and then converts the reflected waves into electrical energy for observation.

At first all of these echo-ranging devices were built on a searchlight principle. The transducer sending out the pulses through the water was moved back and forth like a searchlight to catch the sound waves. As the search-

29

light crossed the target, the bearings could be measured and ranges recorded. But a long time was needed to search through an entire circle with a single transducer. Early in World War II, United States Navy scientists learned that a cylinder could be built of staves, or sections, each of which was a transducer. Sound waves could then be sent in all directions at once. Electronic circuits were also added so that the signals of two or more transducer sections could be formed into a beam. The result was a scanning sonar with electronic beam rotation, which could be used for rapid searching.

In the early 1960s, more refined sonars were developed that could pick up enough detail to create crude images of underwater features on a televisionlike screen. One of these instruments was used in 1963 during the search for the wreckage of nuclear submarine *Thresher*, which mysteriously broke up while test diving in deep water with the loss of all hands. The sound projector (the transducer) was towed above the ocean bottom while emitting narrow, fan-shaped beams of ultrasound. Echoes from the wreckage came back a little sooner than those from the ocean floor. This difference in the time of the echo's return was translated into shadows on the operator's screen, giving a picture of the sea floor and the wreckage similar to one made by a television camera.

Sonar systems can be either active or passive. Active

sonar systems are used chiefly by surface vessels in anti-submarine warfare. Passive systems are used primarily by submarines to detect and evade enemy surface vessels. In an active system, the surface vessel both sends and receives the signal, while in a passive system the submarine does not transmit a signal (which might reveal its presence) but merely listens to the noises made by the surface ships.

The United States Navy and Coast Guard use passive sonar systems in other ways too. Small buoys are equipped with a radio transmitter. Underwater signals—from an enemy submarine, for example—picked up by these radiosonic buoys (usually called "sonobuoys") are automatically transmitted to distant ships and aircraft on patrol duty. In this way, a much greater area can be patrolled effectively against enemy infiltrators.

Navy frogmen use sonar equipment to locate underwater objects such as lost equipment and wrecks. These lightweight, economical, diver-held sonars are powered by standard flashlight batteries. A set of earphones provides the diver with audio information on objects detected by the searching sonar beam.

The frequencies most used in sonar systems range from 5000 to 50,000 cycles per second. The speed at which these signals travel through the water varies with water temperature. At 30 degrees Fahrenheit, for example, the

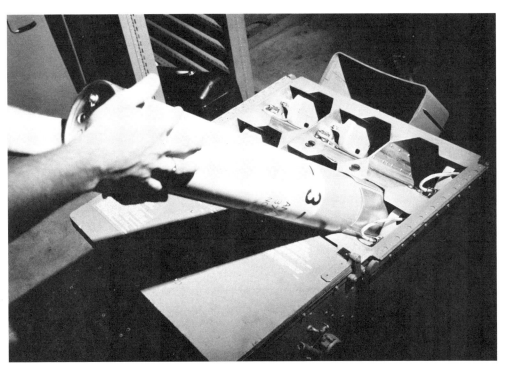

velocity is about 4700 feet per second; at 85 degrees, it increases to about 5000 feet per second. Therefore, in order to calibrate sonar receivers accurately and avoid false readings, thermographic devices must first be lowered into the water to measure the temperature at different depths.

In peacetime, sonar helps navigators make soundings, that is, measure the depth of the ocean. To do so, a type of sonar called a "fathometer" is employed. An operator aboard a ship beams an ultrasonic wave straight down into the water to the ocean floor. The time it takes for the echo of the sound wave to return to the instrument on the ship gives the operator the depth of the water, since the speed of the waves through the water is known. The fathometer measures ocean depths in fathoms; one fathom equals six feet.

In the early 1960s, a West Coast engineer named Wayne Ross developed a more sensitive sonar than those used in World War II. Now known generally as an echo

Top: A crewman aboard a Navy patrol aircraft loads a sonobuoy into an ejector during a training flight. Once in the water, it can pick up signals from an enemy submarine and radio them back to the plane.
Bottom: A frogman tests a portable sonar unit for locating underwater objects.

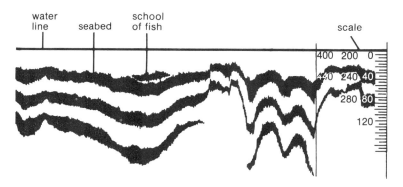

water line   seabed   school of fish   scale

400 200 0
440 240 40
280 80
120

Top: A fish-finder like this one enables commercial fishermen to make use of ultrasonic techniques. The unit provides a permanent record of the contour of the sea bottom as well as locations of schools of fish. Bottom: A typical record.

34

sounder, this improved device was able to locate schools of fish. Operators could also identify the kind of fish by determining the size of the school and depth at which it was swimming. These fish-finders have become a boon for commercial fishermen, increasing the size of their catches. The echo sounder is also important in the navigation of narrow, rocky channels; the echoes bounce back from hidden shoals and angular coastlines.

In the basic echo sounder, an ultrasonic beam can be sent in any direction through the water; the pattern of the echoes is then displayed on a screen, much like blips on a radarscope. The echo sounder also records information in two other ways. The returning echoes are translated into audible sound over a loudspeaker. These sounds can be interpreted by an experienced operator. Hard, clipped *pings* mean the signal is bouncing off a solid wall. Sounds from a hidden sandbar or reef, however, are drawn out, as if someone were scratching a rock with his fingernails. When a permanent record is desired, automatic pen-and-ink soundgrams are made of all the echoes that appear on the screen and the sounds that are heard over the speaker.

In the field of oceanography, echo sounders are invaluable for exploring the ocean floor, making hydrographic surveys, recording distance measurements, and charting fish migrations. For deep soundings, the ultra-

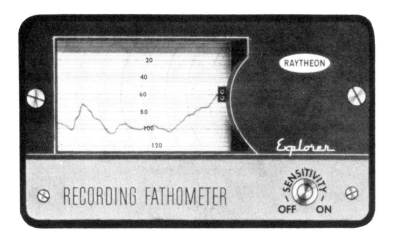

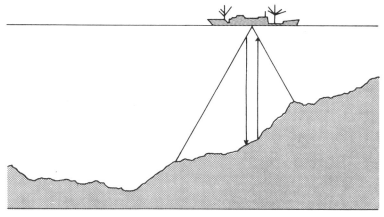

A sonic pulse transmitted by an echo sounder travels down to the ocean floor and is reflected back to the ship. The instrument measures the time elapsed from the instant the pulse leaves until the echo is received. This elapsed time is then automatically translated into a depth reading. On top is a typical fathometer, which measures ocean depths in fathoms.

sonic signals are usually generated by ammonium dihydrogen phosphate crystals; for shallow harbor and river soundings, barium titanate crystals are used.

An echo sounder installed on an oceanographic vessel functions automatically, periodically transmitting an ultrasonic signal of suitable intensity and duration. The signal is directed vertically down into the water. The time interval between the transmission of the signal and reception of the echo is a measure of the water's depth. Depths of up to 6000 fathoms (nearly 7 miles) can be charted with great accuracy.

3

In Science and Industry

Ultrasonics experts and engineers have already found dozens of applications for ultrasound energy in research and industry, but these ideas are all of fairly recent origin.

Just a few years ago, scientists were experimenting with the amazing effects produced by ultrasonic waves. Such experiments were often done with a dish of oil, in which a crystal with metal plates attached was immersed. To the plates were fastened wires from an electrical generating source. As the current was switched on, the plates vibrated at high frequency, sending out ultrasonic waves through the oil. (The reason oil was used as a medium is that it conducts ultrasonic energy well—far better than air.) Soon the oil bubbled, frothed, and produced a fountain effect. Carrying the experiment further, a small glass rod, pointed at one end, was dipped into the oil from above so that it touched the metal plates. Thus, the glass rod was incorporated into the vibratory effects of the ultrasonic waves. If a piece of wood was held against the rod, a hole soon would be burned into it due to friction in the wood fibers set up by the ultrasonic vibrations.

To the scientists performing such experiments, the evidence showed an amazingly powerful force at work. But where was it coming from? Obviously the source was the metal plates moving back and forth, vibrating, through distances of only ten thousandths of an inch. In fact, they were vibrating so fast that to the human eye, which cannot register such rapid movement, they appeared to be standing still. Yet they were changing their vibrational direction at the terrific rate of hundreds of times per second. An object traveling into space at such a rate of speed would be about one million miles away from Earth in just a few seconds. The great rapidity of these vibrations is what not only creates ultrasonic waves but also imparts to them their great power in an effective medium. During recent years, science and industry have made great strides in harnessing this power.

One early industrial device was called a "reflecto-scope." It sent short bursts of ultrasound into a metal object such as a forging or casting to search out flaws. Today these devices are generally known as flaw detectors, and they have become highly sophisticated in their design. Basically, they work on the same principle as the old reflectoscope: A quartz-crystal mechanism is placed against the object to be tested, with only a thin film of oil between them. The oil acts as a couplant, or medium for the more efficient generation of ultrasonic waves. The reflection of the high-frequency beam sent out by the crystal is picked up later by the same crystal, now acting as a microphone. Electronic switching is necessary (as in sonar) because the alternating use of the crystal as transmitter and receiver (actually the transducer with dual capabilities) takes place in millionths of a second.

Top: A modern reflectoscope used to search out flaws in industrial parts such as forgings and castings.
Bottom: A portable ultrasonic flaw detector, which operates on the echo-reflection principle. Such small units can operate continuously for ten full hours without a battery recharge, ensuring a full shift of inspection time.

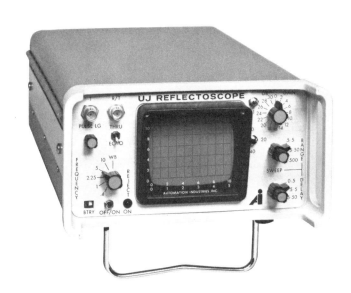

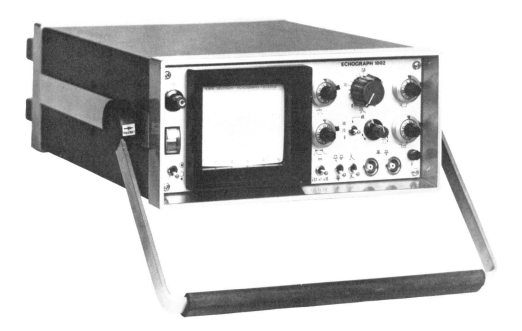

Any flaws in the metal bounce back as echoes and flash on an oscilloscope, showing the location of the defects.

Ultrasonic flaw-detection equipment for industrial testing, inspection, and research—also known as search units—is probably the one method of nondestructive testing that has unlimited possibilities for development. It is considered nondestructive because it does not harm or destroy expensive parts being tested, and it is not dangerous to the operator doing the testing as ultrasonic waves used in this way have no harmful physiological effect. Furthermore, the ultrasonic method improves and extends the flaw-detection abilities of other presently used methods.

By selecting the proper frequency and type of wave, it is possible to investigate most materials—organic, non-organic, and metallic—and to evaluate their surfaces and interiors. Since the attenuation—weakening—of ultrasonic waves is very low in solids or liquids, solid material more than twenty feet thick can be penetrated by either pulsed or continuous waves. Internal flaws in weldments, castings, and forgings can be detected without destruction by either of two methods using pulsed energy. They are known as the echo-reflection method and the shadow method.

The echo-reflection technique is based on the fact that voids, cracks, shears, and inclusions (foreign bodies in a manufactured part) found in solid materials will reflect different ultrasonic waves because of differences in density and elasticity. This method usually involves a single probe, containing a transmitting and receiving transducer in one unit, and is favored for weldment and casting inspection.

The shadow method, which commonly involves two separate transducers (transmitting and receiving), is used to inspect large forgings and castings. A very weak, shadowy signal (or no signal) reaching the receiving element shows that a flaw is blocking and absorbing the ultrasonic energy.

Nondestructive ultrasonic testing of small and large forgings has become a standard manufacturing practice the world over. The measurement of thickness and the inspection of steel-plate lamination with ultrasound are also common procedure, as is the detection of corrosion in high-pressure piping, ship hulls, and many critical components of chemical and petroleum installations.

Ultrasonic thickness gauges can measure many materials simply, accurately, and rapidly from just one side of the part being inspected. They use a pulse-echo technique similar to sonar, in which a sound pulse travels through the material, bounces off the back surface, and travels back through the part. The receiving gauges measure the transit time, compensate for the correct sound velocity of the material, and present a digital readout of the thickness. The operator, using a liquid couplant, merely places the transducer in contact with the part and almost instantly reads the thickness on the digital display.

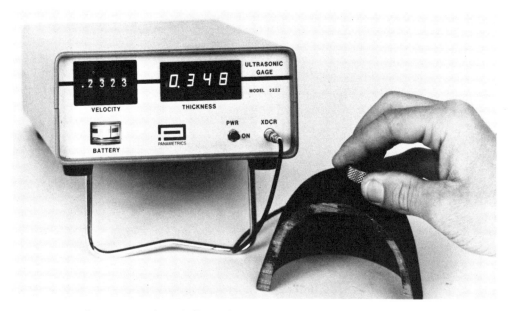

A cast-metal and fiber-glass thickness gauge. This model can measure up to three inches or more of cast metals and up to three-quarters of an inch of fiber glass and rubber.

Opposite, top: A naval architect checks the uniform thickness of a fiber-glass boat hull.

Bottom: Specialized thickness gauges are used to measure metal pipe, tanks, and other parts subject to corrosion. Here an engineer makes an on-site inspection of corroded boiler tubes.

Ultrasonic thickness measurements can be made on most materials including metals, glass, ceramic, liquids, and rubber. They are also effective on fiber-glass boat hulls. And critical dimensions of contact lenses can be measured to insure a correct and comfortable fit to the wearer's corneal curves.

The thickness range to be measured depends on the type of material in question, its shape and surface conditions, as well as the gauge and transducer chosen. Many manufacturers of this equipment claim that calibrated accuracies of up to .0001 of an inch in metal and .001 of an inch in plastic are obtainable.

Flaw-detection and thickness-gauge ultrasonic units have found other profitable applications as well. Many railroads continually check their rail systems with ultrasonic gauges to identify flaws that might cause derailments and other accidents. New ultrasonic devices are also being employed to measure the thickness of concrete structures and to calculate their quality. This work is done by measuring the sound velocity, which is about 12,000 feet per second in high-grade concrete and about half that in poor or deteriorated concrete. Farmers can use a flaw-detection unit to indicate the thickness of fat layers on cattle and pigs and, thus, to determine their marketability. Flaws in automobile tires can be discovered with a similar unit.

A portable ultrasonic degreaser, showing cutaway view of internal parts. Top right, a grease-clogged bearing section is immersed in the degreasing unit. Below, seconds later, the bearing is raised from the bath clean and ready for drying.

The largest commercial application of ultrasound is in cleaning, processing, and degreasing parts and assemblies, especially the cleaning of complicated designs in the automotive, aircraft, and electronics industries.

47

Ultrasonic energy also is widely used to clean optical, dental, surgical, and other precision instruments, as well as dental bridges and dentures. Quicker and better laundering of fabrics is another very practical use of ultrasonics. The intense vibrations break down the attraction between dirt particles and fabrics and literally shake the grime loose. Unlike nondestructive techniques in flaw

An automatic ultrasonic system for cleaning, rinsing, and drying surgical instruments prior to sterilization. Such units are now standard equipment in large hospitals.

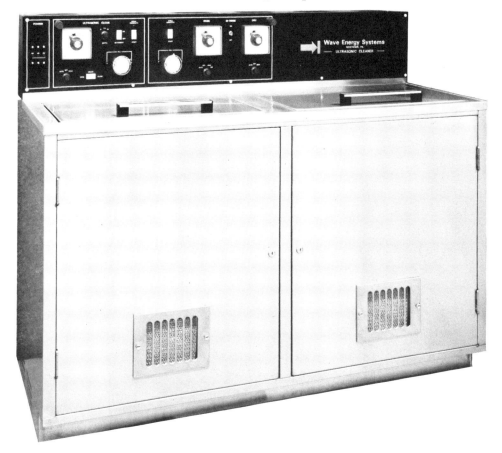

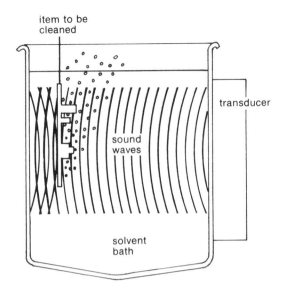

item to be cleaned

transducer

sound waves

solvent bath

How the cavitation effect works: Ultrasonic waves agitate the solvent bath, producing cavities, or microbubbles, which collapse and emit powerful shock waves. These waves jar and loosen dirt on the item to be cleaned.

detection, ultrasonic cleaning is *destructive* for it is based on the cavitation effect.

Cavitation occurs when high-frequency sound waves are passed through cleaning-solvent baths in which the parts or instruments to be cleaned are placed. The ultrasonic waves bring about accelerated movement in the liquid cleaner. This action then produces cavities, or microscopic bubbles, that collapse and send out innumerable tiny but powerful shock waves. These high-energy waves jar and loosen the dirt particles, scrubbing off any grease, dirt, paint, soil, scale, rust, or other contaminations on metal, plastics, or ceramics. Since transducers can be mounted on all sides of cleaning tanks, even the most

A small cleaning unit for removing tarnish and grime from old silver, diamonds and other gems, eyeglass frames, rings, brooches, and delicate jewelry settings. Since many old gem-stones are held in place by dirt in their settings, the unit can discover a loose setting before the stone is lost.

Opposite: Glue residue being removed from cast-iron molds for soft-drink bottles by an ultrasonic cleaner.

complex parts, corners, depressions, and innermost surface areas can be thoroughly cleaned. Such intricate
mechanisms as watch movements, computer memory sections, and shaver heads for electric razors can be rapidly
cleaned in this way.

Instead of spending hours taking intricate clockwork apart
to clean it, jewelers can now clean whole movements ultrasonically. Cavitational microbubbles penetrate everywhere and
remove years of embedded dirt in seconds.
Opposite: A section of computer memory being dipped into
the bath of an ultrasonic cleaning unit. With large cleaning
units such as this one, operators wear precautionary ear pro-
tectors because of the high-frequency tones produced.

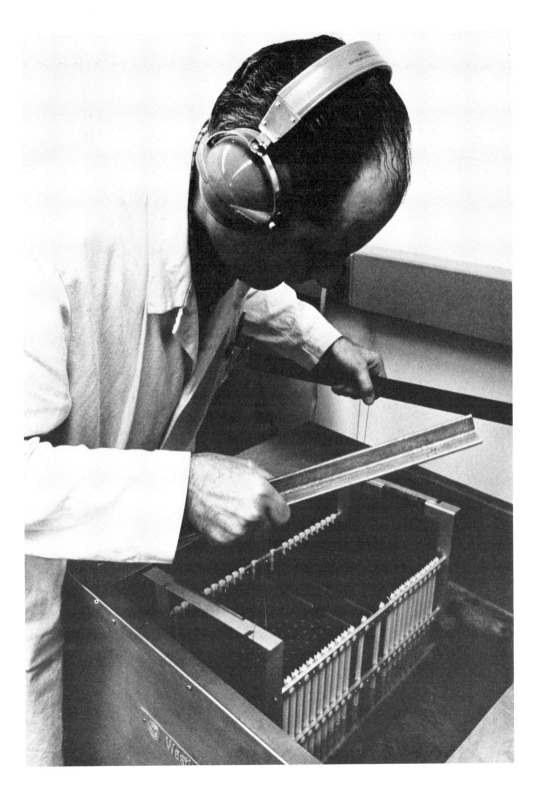

Piezoelectric and magnetostrictive transducers with large radiating areas are used in ultrasonic cleaning. They can produce high-energy frequencies ranging from a faintly audible 15,000 cycles per second (15 kilocycles) to 2,000,000 cycles per second (2 megacycles). The cleaning solutions may be detergents, organic solvents of acid, alkaline types, or even plain water.

Watertight immersion transducers are available where cleaning or flaw-detection must be done underwater or in various industrial liquids. Immersion transducers are also used in ultrasonic holography, where an object to be studied or tested is immersed in a liquid. An interference pattern between two ultrasonic waves (produced by two or more transducers) is used to reconstruct an image of the interior of an opaque object for photographing. The word *holographic* means "a written record of," in this case, a photographic one.

Ultrasonic units are in wide industrial use for welding, bonding, jointing and joining, sealing, assembling, and inserting operations. The intense vibration of an ultrasonic welding head and the material to be welded produce pressure and heat that can weld a thin sheet of metal to a much thicker section. In the same fashion, similar and dissimilar plastics of equal or unequal thickness can be successfuly joined together. Bonding of two identical or dissimilar metals can also be accomplished by ultrasound. A similar application in electronic work is the attaching of gold or aluminum wire leads to semi-conductor devices. Ultrasonic sealing units are commonly used to seal thermoplastic packaging films by applying vibratory mechanical pressure to develop localized heat that melts and fuses the plastic surfaces.

The fast-growing ultrasonic plastics welding industry, in particular, has become big business in the United States and other highly industrialized countries. Welding units send high-intensity ultrasonic vibrations from the tip of a tuned length of metal (aluminum or titanium) called a "horn" through one half of a plastic assembly to the surface that mates with the other half. Frictional heat generated at the interface (the boundary between the two surfaces) creates an even flow of molten plastic throughout the joint. When the molten plastic solidifies, a cohesive bond results.

This process is used on products with two or more plastic components. Applications are multiplying swiftly in the automotive, electronic, small appliance, cosmetic, toy, housewares, and furniture industries. While most of these procedures require large welding units, small, portable ultrasonic welders are coming into wide use for spot welding, bonding vinyl upholstery, film sealing, and many other small jobs.

The concentrated energy of ultrasonic waves is also

employed to insert metal parts into plastic forms for assembling various products. The basic operation is shown in the accompanying drawing. A metal insert, such as a terminal or a screw fastening, is ultrasonically placed in a molded or machined hole that is slightly smaller than the insert. The horn tip of the transducer, changing electric energy to ultrasound, causes frictional heat that melts the plastic at the interface juncture. The melt permits the insert to be driven into place; the plastic then solidifies and re-forms around the threads to encapsulate the in-

How ultrasound is used to insert metal parts into plastic: (1) Metal fastener, held in the horn element, is vibrating at ultrasonic frequency. (2) Vibrations cause surrounding plastic to soften, and fastener is easily inserted. (3) When horn is removed, plastic cools and fastener is sealed into place.

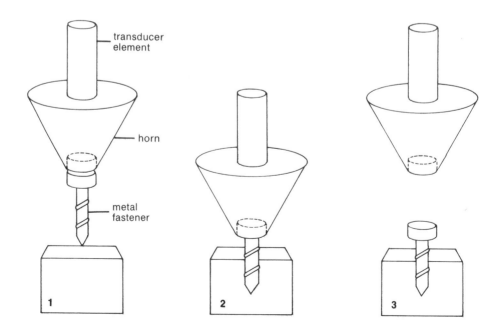

transducer element

horn

metal fastener

1

2

3

sert. Other inserts that can be driven ultrasonically include bushings, handles, pivots, hubs, binding posts, and decorative attachments.

A similar ultrasonic process for joining and assembling metal and plastic is called "staking," or "heading." A hole in the metal part receives a plastic rivet or stud. An especially contoured horn then contacts the rivet, which melts and re-forms as a mushroom-shaped locking head due to friction generated ultrasonically. Tight assemblies are assured because the re-formed stud is allowed to cool under pressure, thus eliminating material memory (return of material to original shape). A clean head, or stage, is formed because no plastic sticks to the horn, which remains relatively cool. Ultrasonic staking is used to put together automobile dashboard clusters and taillight assemblies, as well as a broad range of components for the appliance industry, including radio and television panels.

To drill ultrasonically, an ultrasonic impact grinder is attached to a transducer. The actual cutting or drilling is done by abrasive material, such as silicon carbide or aluminum oxide, which is fed to the cutting face in liquid form. In one type of drill, a magnetostrictive transducer is attached to a tapered cone, or horn. With the appropriate tool at the end of the horn and abrasive liquid, a hole of practically any shape (not just circular) can

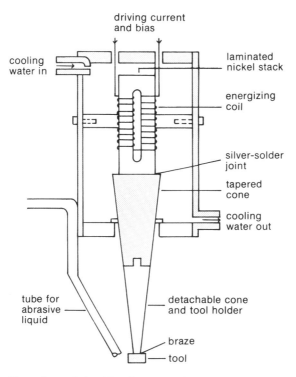

driving current
and bias

cooling
water in

laminated
nickel stack

energizing
coil

silver-solder
joint

tapered
cone

cooling
water out

tube for
abrasive
liquid

detachable cone
and tool holder

braze

tool

Drawing of the "business end" of an ultrasonic drill. Magneto-strictive transducer is attached to the tapered cone, or horn. With the right tool at the end of the horn and with abrasive liquid fed to it, practically any shape of hole can be drilled in gems and hard alloys.

be drilled in hard, brittle materials like tungsten carbide and gems.

Ultrasonic soldering irons are becoming increasingly preferred over the old electric type. In the ultrasonic version, heat is combined with high-frequency vibrations to induce cavitation in molten solder. This process removes oxides from the joint or surface to be soldered, eliminating the need for soldering flux.

Scientists have found that very-high-frequency sound waves can make two liquids that ordinarily would not mix emulsify (dispersion of the fine particles of one liquid in another liquid). For example, alloys of aluminum and lead, iron and lead, and aluminum and cadmium can be made to mix in a liquid state and kept mixed until they solidify. In this way, newer, tougher bearing materials are being created, which can withstand high wear and tear. This production of emulsions is called "ultrasonic material dispersion." Another application of this effect is to render photographic emulsions stable and of the same consistency throughout.

Still another use is the homogenization of milk. Ultrasound is used to break up fat globules, making the fat mix with the milk itself. Pasteurization, the process by which harmful bacteria and other microorganisms are removed from milk, is also commonly done ultrasonically.

Industry is presently making good use of ultrasonic coagulation. This technique bonds, or coagulates, solid or liquid particles present in mist, dust, and smoke into larger clumps, or aggregates. For example, factories that make lampblack, an ingredient of paints, varnishes, and some inks, have installed ultrasonic generators in the flues of their smokestacks. The ultrasonic energy causes the lampblack particles to coagulate, and, becoming heavier than air, they drop down into dispensers instead of escaping to pollute the atmosphere. These units are sometimes called "ultrasonic scrubbers," and many industries use them to clean up their polluted air. In addition, the ultrasonic coagulation effect has been used experimentally around airports and harbors to disperse fog and mist.

Chemical engineers have found that some kinds of chemical reactions are speeded up under the influence of high-energy ultrasonic waves. This property of ultrasound has resulted in a new field called "sono-chemistry." It has been of great use in laboratory work where time is of the essence. Ultrasound has also been employed to break up long-chain polymers—molecules with a highly complicated structure. Such molecular "downgrading," as it is termed, has resulted in the development of new plastic materials for industrial use.

In widespread commercial use today is the ultrasonic level detector. An ultrasonic transmitter and receiver are set into one wall of a tank or container into which a chemical fluid is being poured. While the level of the fluid is below the ultrasonic beam, the beam continues to be reflected off the opposite wall and through air. But when the level of the fluid reaches beam height, reflection of the waves occurs in the fluid instead of in the air above it. As a result, the elapsed time of the pulses traveling across the tank becomes shorter, triggering an electronic shut-off device to stop further pouring of fluid into the tank. Or, if the fluid is being drained off for use elsewhere and its level drops below the beam again, a turn-on device is activated and pouring reoccurs. Thus, the level of the fluid is constantly maintained at the desired height.

Highly sophisticated ultrasonic level detectors are now used by many airlines. They are installed in the fuel tanks of the aircraft to alert the pilot of a sudden fuel shortage, perhaps caused by leakage. Automatic fuel turn-on equipment then goes into action, cutting in the emergency tanks to maintain the fuel level.

So varied are the uses of ultrasound that applications have been found in such widely diverse fields as communications and agriculture. If you listen to phone-in talk shows on radio, you may have heard the show's host mention that his station transmits its signal on a seven- or ten-second delay. This interval allows the station to monitor and cut off a caller who uses indiscreet language before he is heard on the air. It is often accomplished by an ultrasonic delay line, in which the propagation time of sound through a medium such as fused quartz or mercury is used to delay the signal. What happens is that the radio input signal is first fed into the medium, bounced back and forth between two transducers to produce the

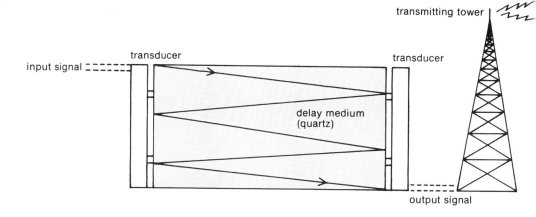

input signal

transducer

transmitting tower

transducer

delay medium
(quartz)

output signal

Radio phone-in shows often use ultrasonics to create a seven- or ten-second delay in transmission. The signal is bounced back and forth between transducers in a delay medium before it is transmitted.

seven- or ten-second delay, after which it is released and broadcast.

In agriculture, use is made of the fact that ultrasonic waves can affect living matter, although the reason is still somewhat obscure. Seeds, for example, have been subjected to ultrasound. In one case it was found that potato plants so treated blossomed a week ahead of their normal time and their yield increased 50 percent.

The fruitful uses of ultrasound seem to go on and on. Burglar alarm systems have been developed that operate on principles similar to those used in the "electric eye." The intruder trips an ultrasonic beam, which in turn sets off an alarm or even notifies the police. These systems have the advantages of invisibility, since the trigger is a sound beam, and easy concealment, since the accessory equipment is made up of tiny transducers.

The United States Air Force is presently using ultrasound in conjunction with radar to train its pilots and crewmen. In this trainer, ultrasonic waves are directed against a molded relief map underwater to simulate responses that occur in actual radar operation during flight over the terrain represented by the map.

In Biology and Medicine

Early in 1950, a United States patent was issued for an ultrasonic device that helps blind people avoid obstacles in their path. It operates by means of echolocation, locating objects with emission of sound pulses and interpretation of the echoes when they return. The pulsed waves are sent out from a mechanism installed in a cane carried by the sightless person. Echoes from any object ahead of him are picked up by a receiver in the cane.

Their energy is then converted by a small transducer into electric impulses that travel by wire to the person's ear, where they are converted into audible sound by means of a special microphone, thereby warning the person of an obstacle ahead.

In medicine, perhaps the most dramatic application of echolocation is in delicate eye surgery. A pioneer in this field is Dr. Nathaniel R. Bronson. In 1959, he had to probe blindly into the eye of a young boy. A sliver from an exploding shotgun shell had been driven deep into the eyeball and had lodged well below the surface—but where? Bronson followed the standard technique of the time. He tried to find the sliver with an electromagnet—and failed. Dr. Bronson had no way of knowing whether the sliver was iron or steel and, therefore, magnetic. It might have been a nonmagnetic brass chip from the shell casing or a tiny piece of concrete from the sidewalk the boy had been playing on.

After cautiously trying other techniques without success, Dr. Bronson, aware that further probing would only cause more harm, reluctantly abandoned any more attempts. Six months later, as he feared, the boy's eye had to be removed. After the eye was dissected, Bronson found out what it was that he had been unable to locate in the living eye: a tiny brass splinter from the shotgun shell casing. Frustrated and saddened, Dr. Bronson felt

65

impelled to search for new ways of locating and removing foreign objects imbedded in human tissue.

At length, Bronson combined two new medical developments to solve his problem. The first was a tiny forceps, devised by an American named Dr. Harvey Thorpe, which could grasp very small objects easily and accurately. The other was a suggestion by a Finnish scientist named Arvo Oksala to use a sonar beam to "see" inside the eye. Using war-surplus electronic components, Bronson assembled a sonar that could explore the eye from the outside. Then he devised a combination sonar-transducer-and-probe (with the forceps) small enough to operate inside the minuscule incisions used in eye surgery. To it was hooked up a small oscilloscope screen across which the sonar echoes flashed.

Using small animals, Bronson tested the probe on every bit of matter that could conceivably get lodged in a human eye—copper, stone, wood, wire, glass, even quartz. Since quartz reflects sound waves just about as well as human tissue does, it proved to be the toughest material to distinguish with his sonar-echolocation device. Then, in September, 1964, Bronson's instrument was used successfully on a human being for the first time. At Walter Reed Hospital outside Washington, D.C., the combination of tiny probe and sonar removed a quarter-inch brass sliver from the eye of an eleven-year-old boy.

As shown in the accompanying diagram, the surgery-by-sonar technique developed by Dr. Bronson permits a surgeon to "see" when extracting foreign particles embedded deep in the eyeball. The tiny sonar-equipped forceps (top) emits an ultrasonic beam, which bounces echoes off the tip of the thin pincers as well as the foreign body. While the surgeon probes the eyeball (below), the echoes are recorded as blips on the oscilloscope screen. As the miniature transducer-probe approaches the foreign object, the echo peak comes closer and closer to the peak of the sound wave (the probe-tip echo) created at the

Developed by Dr. Nathaniel Bronson in the mid-1960s, the surgery-by-sonar technique enables surgeons to "see" when extracting foreign bodies embedded deep in the eyeball.

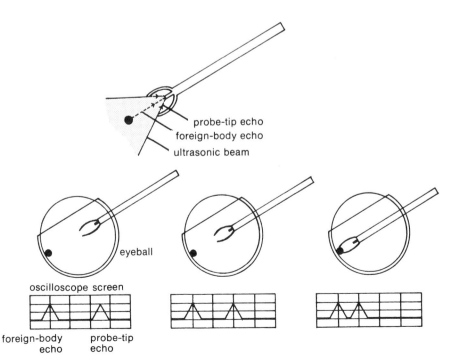

probe-tip echo
foreign-body echo
ultrasonic beam

eyeball

oscilloscope screen

foreign-body
echo

probe-tip
echo

edge of the oscilloscope screen. When the two peaks touch, the surgeon knows that the probe is next to the offending object. At this point, he can release the tiny forceps attached to the probe to grasp the foreign body and extract it.

While Dr. Bronson was developing his instrument in the mid-1960s other ultrasonic applications in medical diagnosis and therapy were being tested rather successfully in Europe. Many startling results were reported, but properly controlled experiments were still needed before the true value of these techniques could be established. For example, as seen in the accompanying diagram, it was shown that living cells might be literally shaken to pieces by a beamed cavitation effect. Further experiments revealed that this effect *did* destroy cells (such as cancer cells), but it appeared to do so nonselectively. Therefore, its usefulness in actual therapy was doubtful.

Yet, as the 1960s progressed, surgeons experimenting with dogs and rabbits succeeded in shattering gallstones into fragments in just a few seconds. The tissues around the gallstones were not damaged, and the fragments of the stones were easily eliminated. In these operations, the ultrasonic beam was transmitted through water, which is elastic. Living tissue is also elastic—it seems to roll with the punch, as it were—stretching rather than splitting under the impact of the ultrasound. Only the gall-

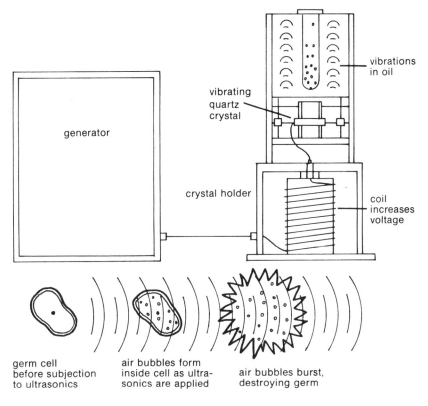

generator

vibrations
in oil

vibrating
quartz
crystal

crystal holder

coil
increases
voltage

germ cell
before subjection
to ultrasonics

air bubbles form
inside cell as ultra-
sonics are applied

air bubbles burst,
destroying germ

How ultrasound can kill germs: Cells can literally be shaken to pieces by a beamed cavitation effect.

stones were broken into small pieces. It was also noted during this period that ultrasonic heat (resulting from the energy absorption and friction caused by the rapid vibrations between cells and between fibrous body tissues) produced many favorable clinical results in the treatment of various forms of arthritis, bursitis, lumbago, and similar ailments.

With the advent of the 1970s, the medical use of ultrasound advanced by leaps and bounds, especially in diagnosis. It has been successful in the detection of solid foreign objects in the body, such as gallstones, kidney stones, and inclusions, and in determining pregnancies as early as five weeks after conception. Distinguishing between malignant tumors and healthy tissues has also been successful in many cases.

Under controlled conditions, ultrasound does not alter the physiology of the tissues but can provide a description of parts of the patient's body as small as .004 of an inch (0.1 of a millimeter) in size. This capability enables the physician to diagnose those parts and judge the relationship of one part to another.

Using ultrasonic instruments for diagnosis is a painless and safe procedure. Unlike X rays, which require special precautions such as lead shielding to prevent damage to healthy tissue, ultrasonic waves cause no harm. Moreover, the small, portable ultrasonic units can be used in the hospital, at the doctor's office, or at the patient's bedside at home.

Here is how ultrasonic diagnosis works: The examination is carried out by coating the skin with any fluid agent that is capable of transmitting sound and excluding air. This step is necessary because air will not conduct ultrasonic waves efficiently; therefore, a conducting medium

A modern portable ultrasonic imaging system used in medical diagnosis. This unit provides high-resolution studies for abdominal ultrasonography as well as obstetric and gynecological applications.

or couplant must be used between the transducer and tissue. Often ordinary mineral oil is used for this purpose, but increasingly newly developed fluid couplants designed especially for ultrasonic apparatus are on the market.

Next, the transducer is placed over the area to be examined and moved back and forth over it. The sound

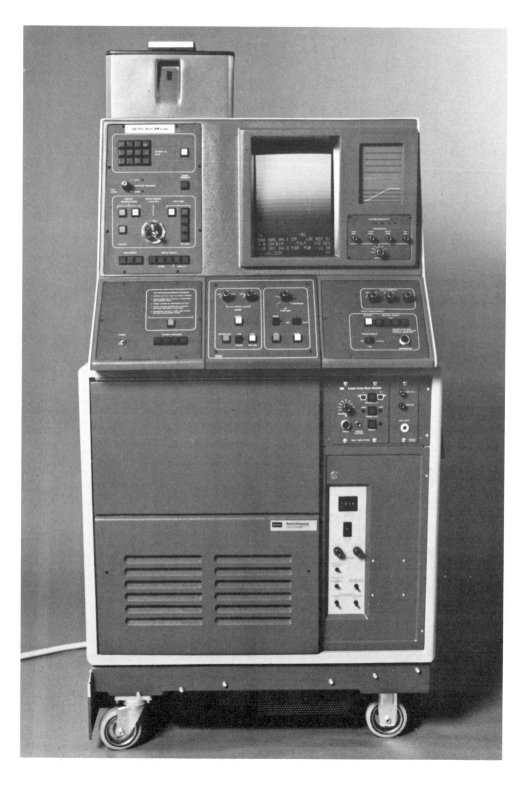

energy produced by the transducer is reflected by the tissues underneath and is reconverted into electrical signals by the same transducer. Then the sound-energy pattern is amplified electronically and displayed on an oscilloscope. This image can be photographed for permanent record and analysis. Ultrasonic recordings called "echograms" can also be taken.

There are several specific uses for ultrasound in medical diagnosis. One is investigation of the area around the eye. Tumors in the skull there can be identified and measured, and the path of the optic nerve can be scrutinized. Also, the inside of the eyeball can be checked for cataracts, hemorrhages, and other abnormalities.

Ultrasound is useful in heart examinations too. Ultrasonic methods of diagnosing cardiac tumors, valve diseases, and accumulation of fluid surrounding the heart have been of increasing value through the 1970s. The principle underlying this technique is the graphic recording of high-frequency sound waves as they bounce back to the recorder after striking an unusual structure within or outside the heart. This method is often known as echo cardiography. Doctors can also use ultrasound to measure the size of the heart and each of its chambers, which

A large multipurpose ultrasonic imaging system used in medical diagnosis and for echo cardiography.

makes it an important tool in the study of congenital heart disease.

Another diagnostic application of ultrasonics employs the Doppler principle to show the rate and direction of blood flow in the body. The Doppler principle states that the pitch of a sound (the highness or lowness of its frequency) approaching an observer increases, while one that moves away from the observer decreases. Thus, it is possible to tell which way blood is traveling within blood-vessel walls by noting an increase or decrease in the frequency of the ultrasonic recording. Devices designed for this purpose are called "ultrasonic flowmeters."

In obstetrics, examination by ultrasound permits exact measurement of the size of the fetus throughout pregnancy, location of the placenta, and establishment of the position of the abdominal organs of the mother. The technique distinguishes differences in tissue density, and unlike X-ray treatment, which requires special safety precautions, there is no danger in the use of ultrasound. This advantage is most important because certain radiation effects inherent in X rays make this treatment hazardous in the early months of pregnancy.

Knowing the size of the developing fetus is especially valuable near the time of delivery. The size of the baby's head relative to the pelvic outlet is crucial then. A dangerous delivery—a disproportionately large baby and a small pelvic cavity—can be predicted, and steps can be taken to prevent difficulties that might cause damage to the infant and the mother.

In addition to locating the site of the placenta on the wall of the uterus, ultrasound can monitor the baby's heartbeat when the mother is in labor, much like a continuously applied stethoscope. At the same time, the labor contractions of the mother are monitored too. From the two records, the physician receives continuous information about the baby's reaction to the stress of labor.

In the actual procedure, a small transducer is placed low on the abdomen of the mother. The sound pulses are reflected by the tissues underneath. Amplified electronically, the sound-energy pattern (the echogram) is displayed on a cathode-ray screen, where the doctor can monitor it visually or photograph it for the record. This technique, called "ultrasonic imaging," has also been applied with dramatic success to other areas of the body such as the upper abdomen, the liver, the pancreas, the gallbladder, and the kidney.

In recent years, doctors have discovered that ultrasound can pinpoint breast tumors that cannot be picked up by other methods. Unfortunately, instruments that now exist for ultrasonic diagnosis of breast tumors take too long for mass screening, that is, for examining large numbers of women in a relatively short amount of time. At the Weizman Institute in Rehovot, Israel, biomedical engineers have been working for several years to develop a quick-acting instrument for ultrasonic diagnosis. It uses an echolocation technique, which should complement current tests for breast cancer, such as thermography (measurement of variations in skin temperature). When perfected, this apparatus will be able to screen quickly enough so that large numbers of women can be examined. It will also provide a three-dimensional rather than a two-dimensional picture on its scanner scope.

Another new development in ultrasonic diagnosis has been called "burn sonar." Doctors need to know how deep a burn in a patient's flesh is before they can determine how and when treatment should proceed. Until the late 1970s, however, most physicians had to rely on their eyes, scalpels, and experience to deal with burn damage. The newly developed ultrasonic burn sensor has now changed this situation.

The device sends out a pulsed current across a transducer to produce ultrasonic waves. Applied to the human skin, it acts like a submarine sonar, listening for reflected signals, which return and register on a scanner scope. Any discontinuity, such as a boundary between irreparably burned tissue and tissue that can be saved, will send back an echo. The instrument measures the time the echo takes to return and converts it into a distance reading indicating the depth of the burn. Knowing this exact depth, the physician can treat the burn with greater effectiveness. The developers of the device claim that it measures depth to an accuracy of 0.1 or 0.2 of a millimeter.

In the field of ultrasonic therapy (treatment of disease), ultrasound unit applicators, such as the one shown in the photograph on page 78, are now in wide use. In the hands of a qualified operator, they are easy to use, portable and lightweight, and are surprisingly effective in the treatment of pain in joints and muscles. Moreover, application time is only a few minutes, and frequency of treatments varies from once daily to three times per week. In principle, these units induce high-energy ultrasonic vibrations in pained tissues and nerve roots, which causes internal heating and gives patients a soothing "micro-massage."

In the actual treatment, the skin over the painful area is coated with a jellylike couplant. The hand-held applicator (a crystal-to-patient transducer) is then moved in slow, steady, rotary or back-and-forth strokes over the area of involvement at the approximate rate of twenty-four square inches per minute. Most treatments require repetition of strokes for a period of five minutes. A tapered housing in the applicator allows for treatment of

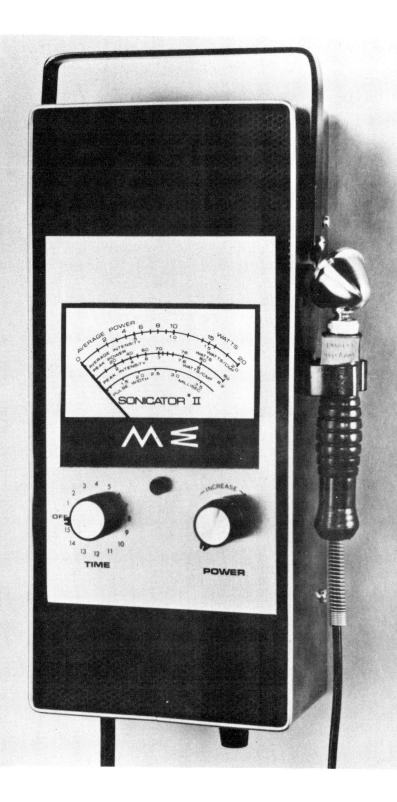

difficult-to-reach regions such as the spaces between toes and fingers.

The list of ailments successfully treated by these units is a long one. They are of benefit to athletes for such injuries as charley horse, sprains and strains, contusions, neuritis, stone bruise, wryneck, scar tissue, adhesions, sciatica, dislocations, shin splints, pulled muscles and tendons, and separations. General conditions treated by ultrasound as an adjunctive therapy include bursitis, myelitis, neuralgia, malignancy, lumbago, rheumatism, arthritis, sciatica, sinitis, post-operative pain, and many more.

While the advantages of ultrasonic therapy are well known and documented, it is possible that in the hands of an unskilled or careless operator the intensity levels of ultrasonic energy produced by this equipment may be surpassed, resulting in tissue injury to patients being so treated. For this reason, the Bureau of Radiological Health of the Food and Drug Administration has issued safety standards to be observed in the use of such equipment. Manufacturers of these units urge their customers to stay well within these standards.

By the end of the 1970s, the acoustic microscope,

Ultrasonic unit applicators are used for therapeutic purposes, such as treatment of pain in joints and muscles.

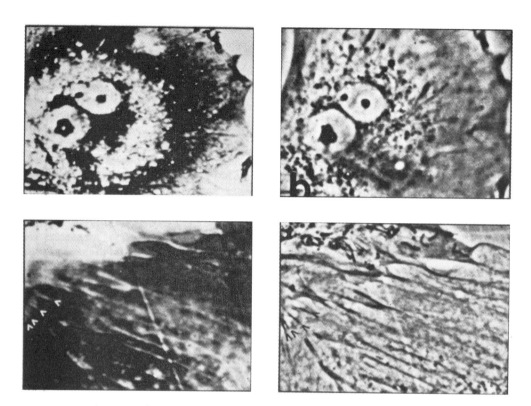

At top, pictures of an embryonic cell with two nuclei; at bottom, pictures show an area of interaction between cells. Pictures on left were taken with the acoustic microscope; pictures on right were taken with a light microscope.

which produces dramatic images with high-frequency sound waves, was substantially improved. In acoustic microscopy, ultrasound enters the living cell and is partially absorbed by structures of differing stiffness or viscosity (areas of ropiness or stickiness). Variations in the acoustic signal are displayed on an imaging screen, which can be photographed for record. The technique can now depict cellular structures as tiny as 0.2 of a micron (one micron is the thousandth part of one millimeter).

Currently scientists in this field are looking at isolated cell components, as well as intact cells, to learn how to interpret the acoustic signal more accurately. Already they can detect minute elements in the nucleus of a cell.

One distinct advantage of the acoustic microscope is that cells do not have to be stained with special dyes (as they must in most light microscopes) to distinguish their components. (See the accompanying photographs.) For example, the familiar bands of human chromosomes seen after staining in a light microscope are visible without staining in an acoustic microscope. A further advantage is that it does no harm to the cells that it examines. The electron microscope, while it has far greater resolution, cannot be used on living cells. (The resolving power of an optical instrument is its ability to form distinguishable images of closely placed objects.)

For a number of years, ultrasonic equipment has been a boon to the field of dentistry. In addition to ultrasonic bath units for the cleaning of dental instruments, there are ultrasonic prophylaxis units for cleaning teeth. They have been used on great numbers of patients with unparalleled comfort, precision, and operating safety. Such a unit needs only a very light touch, and with it the dentist can easily and effectively remove stubborn plaque, calcium deposits, and stains from teeth, leaving crown and root surfaces clean and smooth. Furthermore, the action of the apparatus is so gentle that there is virtually no tissue laceration or bleeding.

Operating on the cavitation principle, the dental prophylaxis unit consists of three major components: an electronic generator, a handpiece assembly, and a set of interchangeable insert tips that touch and clean the teeth. The unit operates by converting ordinary electrical house current into 25,000-cycle current. This power, in turn, is converted by means of a handpiece unit into 25,000 tiny mechanical strokes per second, moving back and forth over a distance of one-thousandth of an inch. Actually, the handpiece contains a magnetostrictive stack transducer that converts the electric power supplied to the handpiece into the ultra-rapid vibrations that activate the insert tip.

Top: An ultrasonic prophylaxis unit for cleaning teeth now in wide use by dentists. Interchangeable activated tips in the handpiece vibrating at ultrasonic frequency are applied to the teeth to clean them.
Bottom: Dentist cleans a patient's teeth with the ultrasonic prophylaxis unit.

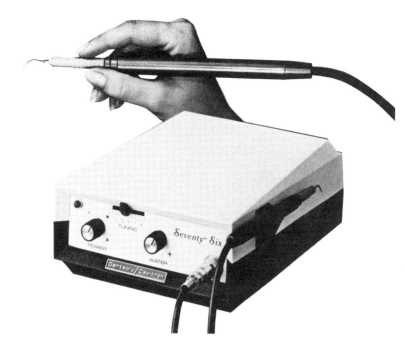

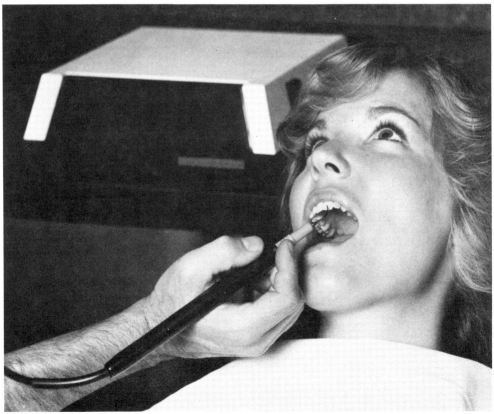

Applied with a water spray and a gentle guiding touch, the activated insert tip, in conjunction with the bubbling action of the water, quickly dislodges material on the patient's teeth. The continuous flow of water is necessary to keep the handpiece cool, and the same water, warmed within the handpiece, is then delivered through the insert and sprayed on the activated tip. The water's flushing action also results in the stimulation and cleansing of the gingiva (the gums), thereby achieving a high level of oral hygiene.

5

The Future

While the existence of ultrasonic energy and its astonishing power has been known for several decades, its development as a separate field has been comparatively recent. After World War II, when ultrasonics received its greatest impetus, scientists were just on the threshold of the potentially fruitful realm of "silent sound." With new technical advances and applications, particularly in the 1970s, that realm has opened up with surprising rapidity. Experts see little reason why even greater progress should not be made in this innovative science in the future. What then is on the horizon for ultrasonics?

In industry and research, the possibilities seem limitless once the high cost of ultrasound equipment is reduced through more efficient methods of mass production. Closer tolerances in the machining of very small and odd-shaped parts will certainly be achieved. New and more efficient techniques will be developed to assemble and package products with ultrasound.

In the field of sono-chemistry, new chemical combinations produced by ultrasonics will make possible undreamed-of molecular rearrangements of long-chain polymers, resulting in more rugged plastics. Ultrasonic flow-meter technology will advance to the stage where pinpoint accuracy will be attained in the cooling systems of delicate machinery, both mechanical and electronic.

As more about the cavitation effect becomes understood, and as better transducers are developed, increasingly efficient cleaning, degreasing, and processing can be carried out with ultrasound. Such advances will benefit the aircraft, automotive, and electronics industries especially.

Advanced cavitation research will also benefit the field of dentistry. In fact, some experts think that the day may come when cavities in teeth can be drilled ultrasonically, with little or no pain to the patient.

Greater mastery and application of the cavitation principle will surely speed the day when ultrasound can be used to disperse fog and smog from airports—and perhaps entire cities as well. At present, the large energy requirement precludes the installation of such systems.

As for the acoustic microscope, scientists are now predicting that it may someday surpass the resolving power of the light microscope. Furthermore, it may provide information about mechanical stress in cellular function, for it seems to be sensitive to slight variations in cell thickness. Also, recent work points to the day when the complete distribution of protein in the human body can be scanned and "read." In the same way, abnormalities in the brain can be charted. Indeed, ultrasound may deliver a completely new picture of what is happening inside the living cell.

Some medical men predict the day when highly concentrated ultrasonic beams will completely replace conventional knives and scalpels in certain kinds of surgery. Such bloodless operations could be performed much more quickly and with less danger to patients.

Brain operations, traditionally long and delicate, are a distinct possibility for ultrasound. In experiments at Columbia University, quartz crystals for special transducers were cut so that the ultrasonic energy could be focused on a particular spot inside the brains of animals. It was found that the energy of such a concentrated beam of ultrasound was as much as 150 times that of an unfocused beam and that it could destroy a preselected diseased brain area in a few seconds.

Much progress is also expected in a brand new field of ultrasonics—chemical extraction. This technique involves the removal by high-intensity ultrasonics of

New ultrasonic probe generator used by chemists, biologists, food technicians, and toxicologists can extract enzymes, oils, and hydrocarbons; disrupt unwanted tissues and cells; accelerate mixing and emulsification; and perform many other tasks in the medicobiology field.

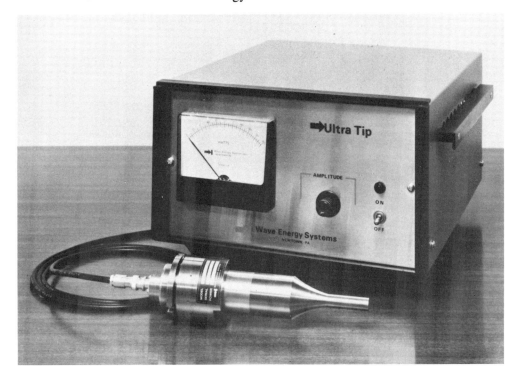

unwanted chemical products called "pharmaceuticals" (alkaloids, glycosides, etc.) from food and drugs. By extracting hydrocarbonlike materials such as waxes from plant crops, yields have been increased. Recently one American ultrasonics firm designed a pilot unit for the Mexican Government to help extract certain resins that were serious contaminants in the guayule shrubs from which rubber is produced.

Already on the market is the ultrasonic probe generator shown in the accompanying photograph. It is designed to extract chemicals such as enzymes, oils and hydrocarbons, and its users include biologists, chemists, food technicians, pharmacologists, and cytologists.

In the words of one ultrasonics engineer, "The future possibilities of ultrasound seem limited by only one factor—the imagination of man."

Index

indicates illustration

ABOUT THE AUTHOR

Born in Glens Falls, New York, David C. Knight received his education both in this country and abroad. He earned his BA degree at Union College in Schenectady, New York, spent a year at the Sorbonne in Paris, then completed his studies at the Engineering Institute in Philadelphia and at the University of Pennsylvania.

Science has been one of Mr. Knight's major interests. He has worked as an editor and production man with Prentice-Hall and for sixteen years served as senior science editor at Franklin Watts. In addition to the many books he has written on scientific subjects, he has contributed a number of science articles to the *New Book of Knowledge*.

Mr. Knight currently lives in Dobbs Ferry, New York, with his wife and two daughters.